His Word *her weapon*

A 21-Day Devotional for Women

Lily,
God loves you.
You were created
for a special purpose.
Healing is yours.
Trust in Him.

Love,
Adreeonah
2020

Adreeonah Mundy

Copyright © 2019 by Adreeonah Mundy
Printed in the United States of America
ISBN: 9781655452192
Independently published

Some Scripture references may be paraphrased version or illustrative references of the author. Unless otherwise specified, all other references are from:

THE HOLY BIBLE, NEW INTERNATIONAL VERSION®, (NIV) ®
Copyright © 1973, 1978, 1984, 2011 by Biblica, Inc.
® Used by permission. All rights reserved worldwide.

NEW AMERICAN STANDARD BIBLE®, (NASB)
Copyright 1960, 1962, 1963,1968,1971,1972,
1973,1975,1977,1995 by The Lockman Foundation.
Used by permission.

NEW KING JAMES VERSION®, (NKJV)
Copyright © 1982 by Thomas Nelson.
Used by permission. All rights reserved.

AMPLIFIED® BIBLE, (AMP)
Copyright © 2015 by The Lockman Foundation
Used by permission.

HOLY BIBLE, New Living Translation, (NLT)
Copyright © 1996, 2004, 2015 by Tyndale House Foundation.
Used by permission of Tyndale House Publishers, Inc., Carol Stream, Illinois 60188.
All rights reserved.

THE CHRISTIAN STANDARD BIBLE. (CSB) Copyright © 2017 by Holman Bible Publishers. Used by permission. Christian Standard Bible®, and CSB® are federally registered trademarks of Holman Bible Publishers, all rights reserved.

Editor - Noleen Arendse
Cover and interior design by Réne Curtis

Dedication

I thought long and hard about who this book—my very first attempt at embracing the writer my YaYa always predicted I would become—should be dedicated to. Inevitably, I decided to dedicate this book to the young woman who finds herself struggling to be the woman God has created her to be.

In hindsight, I realize I spent too much time rehearsing the reasons why I could not write a book and self-publish it, teach a Bible study, or lead women around the world in their walk with God via digital media.

Instead of obsessing over why I could not accomplish these goals, I should've devoted myself to trusting God and simply engaging in one act of obedience at a time.

My fears and self-doubt were all shaped by the lies of the enemy and deep-rooted insecurities from childhood wounds.

But this does not need to be *your* story!

Sis, stop living below your inheritance as a child of God, which makes you a co-heir with Christ.

If you want to be a writer, start writing cause the book won't write itself.

If you want to start the non-profit, write the vision and make it plain.

If you want to become a photographer, buy the camera and practice on anything and anyone.

If you want to act in a show or star in a movie, go out for the audition and you better kill it!

If you want to preach, preach to your friends and the walls until the walls start crumbling down and doors begin to swing open.

If you want to start a business, start writing the business plan and pray, pray, pray.

Whatever it is that you know God has placed inside of you to do, go after it with all your heart. The enemy of your soul will try to stop you at every corner but don't forget your secret weapon, the Sword of the Spirit— The Word of God.

Love,

Adreeonah

Hey girl!

I don't know how you stumbled upon this 21-day devotional, but I want you to know this: It was written with you in mind. I do not take it lightly that you have decided to spend one-on-one time with our Savior through the words I penned during some of the most trying times of my life.

When I dedicated my life to Christ and was introduced to the notion of "quiet time," I used devotionals as a base for my time with God. However, I was often left with a desire to "go deeper." I wanted to look up Scriptures, be asked nitty-gritty questions that would convict or lead to encouragement, cause me to meditate on the Lord, and ponder what He would have me to focus on for that day.

Unfortunately, I didn't always find what I was seeking. I wanted more than just a quick word and one verse of Scripture.

I needed to actually reference my Bible and engage my mind and heart in pursuit of the Lord. After growing in my knowledge and love-relationship with God, I had this thought: "Write the kind of devo you would enjoy reading every morning; one that would challenge you to do more than read and put the book up for the day."

It is my prayer that this devotional expands your knowledge of God and deepens your pursuit of Him through time in the Word and prayer. I have purposely only referenced the Scripture verses each day with high hopes that you will use this devotional as a supplement to your independent study of the Word.

Having shared that, I can't begin to describe how grateful I am for this book to be in your hands. This book of devos represents one of the many desires that I possessed after months of begging God to reveal my purpose. However, this dream that I fought so hard to uncover was almost destroyed before my fingers could hit the keyboard. Why, you may ask?

Things like paralyzing fear, self-doubt, love, unforgiveness, comparison, relational conflict, and insecurities, among so many other things, hit me like a ton of bricks. I began to think, "Who I am to write a devotional? Who will read it? I'm not good enough. I don't have what it takes to help anyone else through their stuff when I'm dealing with my own stuff!" These comments and the problems I listed may look all too familiar to you because they all have one thing in common: They are frequently used weapons of the enemy.

I have experienced the attack of the enemy in many areas of my life, as I am sure you have as well. But, just like my mama likes to say, "What the enemy meant for evil, God meant for good." I was oblivious of it at the time, but the enemy's constant bullying provided me with much needed ammunition. His weapons backfired and are the very reason this book is before you today.

I decided to write out my thoughts, lessons, and most importantly, the weapons (Scriptures) that God placed on my heart to share with you at your point of need.

In this devotional, you will be pushed to deepen your relationship with God through daily reflection of three key Scriptures following each devo and prayer, as well as your ability to look at your life and plan to partner with God to make changes where need be (*these are the "Your Turn" sections*). It is my prayer that after this devotional, you are ready when the devil comes throwing his fiery darts. Sis, you don't have to fear him, run and hide, or surrender to his antics. Why? Because you are equipped with powerful tools.

In Ephesians 6, it always amazes me that the full armor of God is outlined for the believer to suit up with daily, yet the only offensive weapon in the armor is the "Sword of the Spirit, which is the Word of God."

One of my greatest heart's desires is for us to be women who learn to use our most powerful and efficient weapon —the Word of God!

No matter what the situation or circumstance may be, big or small, it is absolutely no match for the unyielding, unbreakable, immovable, infallible, chain-breaking, demon-slaying, Word of God.

But it does not stop with knowing the Word and using the Word. We must also pray. After Paul's exhortation for the people of God to take up the Sword of the Spirit, he says: "Pray at all times in the Spirit with every prayer and request and stay alert with all perseverance and intercession for all the saints." Listen, don't skim past the daily prayers, add to them, and make them your own, ask the Holy Spirit to guide you each day as you go before the Throne of Grace.

Give yourself permission to spend uninterrupted time with the Lord. Even if this means you have to set the alarm clock for an hour earlier, take that lunch break away from your desk without your phone, or go to bed later, do it. Okay, enough of my Sisterly advice. ***You ready? Let's go!!***

Contents

Day 1
God Will Reveal Himself

"O God, you are my God; I earnestly search for you.
My soul thirsts for you; my whole body longs for you
in this parched and weary land where there is no water."

— PSALM 63:1, NLT

E van Roberts, a young Welsh believer who lived in the early 1900s, faithfully attended prayer meetings and Bible classes every night of the week. Sandwiched in, of course, was his own personal prayer and study. For 13 years, Roberts diligently sought the Lord with this hunger and intensity, begging the Lord for a "mighty visitation" of the Holy Spirit.

One day Evan's petitions were answered, and the Lord came in such a mighty way that his experiences with Him were not only unexplainable, but they left Evan trembling uncontrollably at random times throughout the day. Evan was visited every day by the Lord for weeks and he went on to lead one of the greatest revivals in history, "The Welsh Revival."

Psalm 63 is one of my favorite Bible verses. For months, I recited it every morning with tears streaming down my face. I was in a rough patch in my life; living at home again because my apartment was mice-infested and creepy, working at a job that literally made my stomach turn as I approached the parking lot, and feeling as if God was miles away. I craved the presence of God. I needed Him more than I needed breath in my lungs, after all, He is life. David had these same sentiments when he penned this Psalm.

Theologians believe David formulated these words while on the run from Saul or during a brief exile when his own son tried to overthrow him as king. Either way, David was in a valley moment of his life: no palace, no servants, no wives—just himself, soldiers, and God. He very well could have been without actual water but that was not his concern. He longed for living water that would never run dry.

As we grow in our relationship with God, we crave intimacy with Him. Oh, how we long for His presence to be revealed—but how many of us are willing to pray and wait for Him? To sit in silence for as long as we prayed, so prayer can truly be a two-way conversation, versus a monologue.

I must admit, I get just a little bit discouraged thinking about waiting longer than a decade to experience the sweet presence of God. However, I then marvel at how much of a privilege it is for God to answer such a request and I can't help but be humbled and in awe of His greatness, love, mercy, and kindness.

Evan's story is proof that God hears us and when He decides to answer it, it isn't just for our benefit but it's for us to be so impacted, so saturated in His Spirit, that it compels us to share Him with others. You can find out more about Evan's inspiring story at pisgahchapel.com/about/evanroberts.

Prayer

Father God, thank You for loving me enough to reveal parts of Your glory to me at Your discretion. Lord, thank You for Your sweet presence that transforms me and evokes a fire within that cannot be tamed. Lord, I pray for the diligence to be sold out to You and expectant of Your revelation that will come to first to change me and then the world.

In Jesus name, Amen.

Today's Weapons

Matthew 5:6, NIV

_____

_____

_____

_____

Acts 17:27, NIV

_____

_____

_____

_____

1 Chronicles 16:11, NASB

_____

_____

_____

_____

Your Turn

When is the last time you searched for God and truly waited for Him to reveal Himself to you? What feelings did you experience during this time? Did you ever receive the revelation you were seeking, or did you allow your feelings to take authority over your will and strength to wait on God?

Day 2
The Word Of God—Lost

"When the king heard the words of the book
of the law, he tore his clothes."

— 2 KINGS 22:11, NASB

I don't think I've ever been so struck by a book Bible study (*Lord, Teach Me to Study the Bible in 28 Days* by Kay Arthur). Okay, maybe that's a bit dramatic and a slight overstatement, but my study of King Josiah has left a lasting impression on my mind and heart. This morning (or whatever time of the day you are reading this, Sis) I want to share some of the insights I learned from that study.

Josiah became king at the tender age of eight! Yes, you read that right, eight. He reigned over Jerusalem for 31 years.

Unlike his father, Josiah did right in the eyes of the Lord and followed the examples of his ancestors, Hezekiah and David.

In the 18th year of his reign, Josiah sent the high priest, Hilkiah, to the Lord's temple along with his secretary, Shaphan, to alert the gatekeepers (those in charge of the people who entered the temple to give their gifts), to give the silver to the overseers who, in turn, were to give it to the workers to make the proper repairs to the temple of the Lord. While in the temple, Hilkiah found the Book of the Law (possibly the entire Torah or just the book of Deuteronomy).

Upon their return, Hilkiah gave the Book of the Law to Shaphan to read aloud in the hearing of King Josiah. Immediately, King Josiah's heart broke and he tore his clothes, which in those times signified great pain, sorrow, mourning, and repentance. After hearing all the Lord's commands that his forefathers had broken, Josiah's heart was grieved.

Josiah's response to this newfound information was to send some of his trusted men to inquire of the Lord through the prophetess Huldah. The Word from the Lord through Huldah was of impending disaster due to the people's idolatry and blatant disobedience to God's Word.

However, God made it His point to inform Josiah that he would not witness the devastation that He would bring upon Jerusalem. Why? Josiah's tender heart of repentance and humility before the Lord after he heard the truth, the Book of the Law, caused the Lord to show him great mercy and kindness.

Afterward, Josiah went before all of Jerusalem and the inhabitants of Judah and read the Book of the Law. Right there before God and men, King Josiah made a covenant before the Lord to keep His commands and walk in His ways.

The Bible states in 2 Chronicles 34:33, "Josiah removed all the detestable idols from all the territory belonging to the Israelites, and he had all who were present in Israel serve the LORD their God. As long as he lived, they did not fail to follow the LORD, the God of their ancestors."

When I read King Josiah's story, I am in awe of quite a few things: his reign beginning at the age of eight, his integrity before God and heart to pursue Him even when he did not fully know Him, and his instant repentance when God revealed Himself through His written Word.

One question that burned within as I read the story was: How did the Book of the Law become lost in the temple, of all places, in the first place? Had anyone been searching for it? Furthermore, I marvel at Josiah's response to the Word of the Lord upon his very first hearing.

My question for you and for me is:

Do we respond in the same manner?

When we hear the Word of the Lord, are we quick to examine our lives and destroy and "take away all abominations" in it that don't align with the Word of God? Could the Book of the Law, the Word of God, be lost in our own homes?

As I read my Study Bible to prepare this devo, I was struck by these words:

"There is not much difference between

the book hidden in the Temple and

the Bible hidden on the bookshelf.

An unread Bible is as useless as a lost one."

Prayer

God, my God, thank You for Your written Word that penetrates my heart and helps me to follow hard after You. Forgive me of my blatant sins after I know what Your Word says about my actions and that You are not pleased. Help me to be like Josiah, Lord, and wholeheartedly pursue You as well as implore others to do the same. Thank You, Jesus, for Your sweet sacrifice that allows me to come before the Throne of Grace, even when I get it wrong. Put a fire in my heart, O God, to read Your Word daily and for the only place for it to be hidden, is in my heart.

In Your name I pray, Amen.

Today's Weapons

Deuteronomy 13:4, NASB

_____

_____

_____

_____

Matthew 22:37, NIV

_____

_____

_____

_____

Joshua 1:8, NASB

_____

_____

_____

_____

Your Turn

I challenge you to go back and read the entire chapters of **2 Kings 22 and 2 Chronicles 34**. Could the book of the Law, the entire Bible in our time, be lost on your bookshelf? Only you and the Lord know if you take time to read His Word daily. And even for those of us that do, this is only half of the battle.

Only you and He know if you act in ways that reveal that you have, in fact, read it and believe it. I once heard a preacher say, "If you don't live your belief, you don't actually believe it." Examine your life and ask God to show you all the idols and "abominations" that lie within and ask God to help you uproot them all.

Day 3
Is That You, God?

"The Lord came and stood there, calling as at other
times, "Samuel! Samuel!" Then Samuel said,
"Speak, for your servant is listening."

— 1 SAMUEL 3:10, NIV

A few years ago, I accepted a job offer that I thought would be "okay" and a fresh start from where I was. Honestly, I think I traded one hell for another, maybe an even hotter one. The job was *STRESSFUL!* Everything from the level of trauma the children faced, from the overbearing and then some uninvolved families, to the needy and demanding companies I collaborated with... and not to mention the paperwork, oh the paperwork and non-negotiable deadlines. I think you get the picture and I have effectively set the scene.

One day, I was busy working, and things were slow for a change due to me being in the middle of a transition to another site and only being responsible for a small caseload. I was quietly hanging out in my office and when suddenly I felt nudge to, "Go ask Erica if she needs help." Now I have no problem with helping, but I had questions. Where did that come from? So, I sat there... still working, listening to my gospel music, pretending that I didn't hear the Holy Spirit give me marching orders.

After about 45 minutes, "the nudge" just wouldn't let up. I reluctantly relinquished and asked, "Lord do you want me to go now? What if she says she doesn't need any help?" No response just a continual "nudge."

I finally got up enough courage to go find her and simply said, "I sense that you may have a lot to do... can I help you with anything?" Long story short, she shared that she had just come from saying a short prayer asking God to help her meet the demands of the day.

I can still remember one of her statements verbatim, "You are an answered prayer right now." I couldn't believe it! Lil ol' me was used as an answer to someone's prayer. And to think I wasn't going to listen to that gentle whisper.

In our text for the day, young Samuel was oblivious to the voice of the Lord. He did not even consider that the Lord had been calling him, which is apparent in his actions of going to Eli the priest, not once or twice but three times. I assume Samuel thought the voice that was calling him had to be from Eli and not from God Almighty Himself.

The Bible tells us Eli realized it was the Lord and gave Samuel instructions for the next call of the Lord. "Samuel did not yet know the Lord: The word of the Lord had not yet been revealed to him" (1 Samuel 3:7, NIV). This fact provides me with much comfort because it implies that God is the initiator in His revelation to us, His people.

Samuel was getting ready for bed and the Lord decided He was ready to speak with the boy who had been learning the Word of God and living in the temple since he was a baby. God met Samuel in the ordinary ebb and flow of life and did not count it against Samuel that he did not yet know His voice.

I think about the story I shared and how God had shown me the same favor. He initiated our conversation that ordinary day in my small office. I had been seeking Him for months, reading His Word, praying, and nothing. I was not sure how His voice would sound and, at first, like Samuel, I did not recognize it. However, He did not hold it against me when I first questioned, "Is that You, God, or me?" He gave confirmation and I had a choice to make.

Sis, all I want you to get from today is: God speaks and when He does, He's most definitely talking to you, and expecting you to listen. Spend less time with your futile questioning and simply do what He's asking you to do.

You never want to miss an opportunity to be used by God, whether it be big or small. I will always remember the joy I experienced as I sat down at my desk after "completing the mission." I always ask God to use me and He did! And if He can use me, He can most certainly use you too.

Prayer

Dear Lord, thank you for speaking to me several times until I know that it is You and move! Grant me the discernment I need to make wise decisions and be obedient to You in every circumstance. Lord, I want to remember that You want to lead me more than I want to follow. You know how to speak so that I know it is You; help me to trust this truth. I pray that You continue to use me and that I will always be willing to go wherever You lead me.

In Jesus name, Amen.

Today's Weapons

Mark 4:24, NIV

_____

_____

_____

_____

Proverbs 2:1-5, NKJV

_____

_____

_____

_____

Psalm 119:105, NKJV

_____

_____

_____

_____

Your Turn

Can you recall the last time you were "nudged" by the Holy Spirit? What was He asking you to do? Were you able to follow through with His request or did fear come in to bully you into disobedience?

I want you to carefully think about your answers to these questions and decide right here, right now, once and for all, that you will follow the leading of the Holy Spirit, no matter how scary, daunting, or down right crazy the task may seem. Use your daily weapons to stir you up in the Lord and speak back to the enemy when he tries to hinder you again.

Day 4
Death By Comparison

"When Peter saw him, he asked, "Lord, what about him? Jesus answered, "If I want him to remain alive until I return, what is that to you? You must follow me."

— **JOHN 21:21-22, NIV**

A h comparison, the thief of contentment! I would bet my last dollar, if I were a betting woman, that you've probably compared yourself to someone over the span of your lifetime. You may have even done so recently; like yesterday on Instagram, Facebook, at work, or even in the grocery store. It's a fact that when we take our eyes off Jesus, comparison can find its way into our line of sight.

I love how Jesus explained this concept to Peter. Peter had denied Jesus the night before His resurrection and in this passage, we find Jesus resurrected and ready to "reinstate" Peter as a disciple. Jesus takes His time to ask Peter questions and give him insight into his future. And do you know what Peter does? He asks about another person's fate. The resurrected King is literally in front of him and Peter's eyes are elsewhere. If I can take the liberty to paraphrase, this was Jesus' response: "Do not worry about him (John) and what I have planned for his future. Instead, you worry about Me because I am who you follow, who you try to duplicate, and compare to for the purposes of becoming better."

Jesus is not only speaking to Peter in this verse but to every one of us when we decide to get tangled up in the web of comparison. Hear me when I say: *comparison literally kills!* It kills your joy. It kills your dreams. It kills your confidence. Perhaps, more importantly, it kills your assurance of who God created you to be.

What or whom have you been concerned with that has led you to forget about the very thing the Lord has in store for you? Peter was unable to focus on the message Jesus was instilling because of his strong desire to know another man's destiny. In this passage, Jesus tells Peter more than once, "Feed my sheep" (verse 17). What an honor! For Jesus to entrust His precious sheep with anyone, is an indication of His love and trust; that with His help, you are up for such a task.

We know how much Peter had messed up prior to this moment. He had denied Jesus, cut off an ear, shown a lack of faith when walking on water... yet, Jesus still named him the rock on which He'd build His church (**Matthew 6:18**).

Do not allow your concern with what God is doing in the lives of those around you, cause you to miss out on the great things God has planned just for you!

Prayer

Lord, help me to see that I am special in Your sight and created with a distinct and unique purpose. Lord, I pray for a deep understanding of Your will for my life that enables me satisfaction in fulfilling my own destiny while also cheering on others. Thank You that I can look to You for all guidance and inspiration and no one else. I vow to keep my head up and my eyes straight ahead, on You!

In Jesus name, Amen.

Today's Weapons

Galatians 6:4, NKJV

_____

_____

_____

_____

2 Corinthians 10:12, NKJV

_____

_____

_____

_____

1 Thessalonians 4:1, NKJV

_____

_____

_____

_____

Your Turn

Let's face it, if you are anything like me, you compare whether you like it or not. I want us to uproot this dirty truth and cast it into Hell where it belongs. Remember that comparison, jealousy, and coveting is a sin and dishonorable in the sight of God.

Why? It's just as good as saying you don't trust God's plan for YOUR life, that His timing is somehow with error and flaw, and that He is unfair. Don't beat yourself up about it, repent and put a plan in place to combat feelings of comparison and jealousy. One thing I like to do is compliment the person I've been secretly comparing myself to. I also pray for them and invite the Holy Spirit to show me any areas that I could possibly be a blessing to them. You can't quite remain jealous and insecure about a person or things once you have committed them to God in prayer.

Take some time and write out all the ways you've compared your life to that of someone else's. Next, make a list of all the things that you are grateful for that you already have. This list can include attributes, possessions, family, friends, whatever—anything that you know you are grateful to God for. Focus on these things and it will lead to gratitude and, most importantly, praise!

Day 5
As Pure As Gold

But He knows the way that I take;
When He has tested me,
I shall come forth as gold."

— **JOB 23:10, NKJ**

I f you are anything like me, you love gold... a nice gold necklace, ring, watch, earrings, bracelet; you name it, I love it. It's just so shiny, beautiful, and durable... but not without a cost. For gold to be so eye-catching, it must go through an extensive and careful testing and refining process. I once read that gold is refined by "heating it and skimming off the dross over and over again until the reflection of the goldsmith can be seen it." I almost jumped out of my seat upon repeatedly marveling at that statement.

The term "dross" derives from the Old English word "dros," which means the scum and solid impurities produced when smelting metal.

In our case, we pass through the fire and must withstand the horrible, almost unbearable, heat and chipping away at our "dross," that is our flesh and sinful nature, to cleanse us of all our impurities. This painful process is necessary because, in the end, God wants to see a little more of Himself in us. We go through tests just as Job—not because we are being punished but because we are being pruned. We are being tested and refined much like gold.

We often say, "I want to be like Christ. I just want to love others, do the will of the Father, be forgiving, give to the needy, change the world for the glory of God," all great things... but when the tests come, we soon forget what we asked for, now don't we?

Job was a God-fearing upright man. I mean God Himself asked the enemy if he had tried His servant Job (1:8). God was confident in His boasting about Job to Satan because He knew Job was trustworthy and, specifically, the most blameless man walking the Earth at that time. However, even in all Job's faithfulness, he did not fully know God and furthermore did not fully know himself. That is until he was tested.

One of the most famous theologians, John Calvin, put it this way: "Man never attains to a true self-knowledge until he has previously contemplated the face of God, and come down after such contemplation to look into himself."

Job did not fully grasp the character of God until he'd gone through the devastation of life, as he knew it, being ripped out of his hands, causing him to wrestle with the motives of a just God allowing such unjust treatment.

Job began to question God even though in chapter 23, our text for the day, he acknowledges the reason for the test. Job became weary as we have all been guilty of doing.

After his interrogation of God, Job received answers from the Creator that caused him to shudder in humility and acknowledge God for who He is. How can we be so sure? Check out Job's statement in 42:5-6: "I had heard reports about you, but now my eyes have seen you. Therefore, I reject my words and am sorry for them; I am dust and ashes." (CSB) Job could only arrive at this conclusion about God and himself after facing trials that caused him to seek God in ways he had never done before.

Job teaches us the truth that if you seek God in new ways, He will reveal Himself in new ways. Job was afforded the opportunity to deepen his relationship with God through the worst season of his life.

Just like Job, Sis, you and I will endure some painful moments that will be the breeding ground for our faith in God to grow like never before. Just as gold goes through a process of thorough refining and testing, so do we as children of God.

It's not that He needs to know we can be trusted with the great plans He has for our lives and the blessings He is willing and able to bestow upon us. Rather, we need to be assured through some of our most painful valley experiences that God can trust us with the mountaintop because of how we responded in the valley. Like the old church mothers use to say, "We need to know that we know, that we know, that we know." God is control and, *"It's alright even if it ain't alright."*

Are you going through the fire right now? Do you feel like gold—like your "dross is being skimmed off over and over again"? If your answer is yes, just think about how great you are going to appear once you arise from the fire looking a little more like God Himself.

Prayer

Thank You, Lord, that even when I don't understand why the tests come or how I will make it through them, they are only for my good. May I always remember that, as Your child, life will not always be easy, but it will be worthwhile. Every trial I face and successfully endure produces an uncanny resemblance to my Savior and Your Son. Thank you for being compassionate enough to make lil ol' me look a little more like You.

In Jesus name, Amen.

Today's Weapons

2 Corinthians 3:18, KJV

_____

_____

_____

_____

Colossians 3:10, NLT

_____

_____

_____

_____

Romans 8:28, NIV

_____

_____

_____

_____

Your Turn

Is this you right now? Do you feel like you are constantly being put through the fire and unsure of when you will ever find the water you so desperately need to put it out? I want you to firmly say out loud: "This too shall pass. One day I will look more like my Savior and it will all be worth it."

Do me a favor. Grab your Bible and look up all the attributes of God that you can aspire to (loving, righteous, holy, forgiving, discerning, and immovable) and ask God to help you live in the tribulations of today with an acute awareness that they are only preparing you for tomorrow.

Our main goal is to be a little more like Christ daily and this will never be easy on this side of eternity. Stay encouraged, get on your knees and pray like never before. God is with you and one day you will be, "As pure as gold."

Day 6
Wrestle With God

"Then the man said, "Your name will no longer be
Jacob, but Israel because you have struggled
with God and with humans
and have overcome."
— **GENISIS 32:28**

I f we aren't careful, we can often find ourselves defeated and discouraged due to what we perceive are unanswered prayers. Many of us, including myself, do not know what it means to truly wrestle with God in prayer. If I'm being honest, after a certain prayer request is not answered, I'm ready to throw in the towel; ready to give up way too easily. I begin to think, "Well maybe what I'm asking for just isn't in His will."

My youngest brother has a thing for listening to sermons as one of his favorite pastimes and I've had the pleasure of hearing them whether I want to or not. One sermon bears repeating as I think it will accurately illustrate what it looks like to wrestle with God in prayer.

The charismatic pastor preached about a middle-aged woman in his congregation who had been praying and believing God that her wayward son would return home and be saved at her church's tent revival. She had been praying for her son's salvation for years and was adamant that this would be the year that God would hear her cry for help and save him (Psalm 145:19).

In fact, this woman dared to believe so much that she began to tell others about the miracle before it occurred. She predicted her son would be coming with his wife and son on the last night of revival and he would receive salvation.

The pastor, telling the story, admitted to being cynical at the sound of her prophecy and half-heartedly agreed to pray and believe with her.

Despite the opinions of others, this mother continued to pray as she had done for years and she took things a step further by preparing for her son's arrival.

On the last night of the revival, the pastor recalled seeing a truck pull up. The woman began to weep and ran to greet her son who had, in fact, come to be revived and accepted Jesus Christ as his Lord and personal Savior.

I share this story to encourage you, no to charge you, to never give up when it comes to prayer. Go before our Father with expectancy, humility, and persistence. He knows what you need and at the right time, He will supply all of them (Philippians 4:19).

Your job is to keep praying even when you don't feel like it, when nothing around you is changing, and when all looks lost. It is this type of desperation, faith, and tenacity that will cause God to say, "You have struggled with God and with humans and have overcome." Don't be afraid to wrestle with God in prayer!

Prayer

Father God, forgive us for giving up way too easily. Have mercy on our weary souls and fill us with the desire to tarry in prayer, O God. Thank you, God, for the privilege to boldly come before Your throne and actually "win" Your blessings. I will never give up on prayer and belief in Your ability to supply every one of my needs according to Your perfect will for my life.

In Jesus name, Amen.

Today's Weapons

Matthew 7:7

_____

_____

_____

_____

Mark 11:24

_____

_____

_____

_____

Psalm 34:4

_____

_____

_____

_____

Your Turn

What areas have you just given up going to His throne over? Be honest and take an inventory of those unfulfilled dreams, lost people, broken relationships, or whatever specific requests you used to take before the Lord and ask for forgiveness.

Ask for forgiveness for your lack of belief and the strength to continue to "wrestle in prayer" even when there is no answer in sight.

Draft your own prayer using
Today's Weapons:
Matthew 7:7 ; Mark 11:24; Psalm 34:4

_____

_____

_____

_____

_____

_____

_____

_____

_____

_____

_____

_____

_____

_____

_____

_____

_____

_____

_____

_____

_____

_____

_____

_____

Day 7
Unfailing Love

"What a person desires is unfailing love;
better to be poor than a liar."

— PROVERBS 19:22, NIV

I admit, my first encounter with this Scripture left me feeling a bit perplexed. I thought to myself, "What does unfailing love have to do with a poor person and a liar?" However, after Dannah Gresh, author of *Get Lost: Your Guide to Finding True Love*, broke down the meaning of the passage, a lightbulb went off.

Along my purity journey, I had become guilty of denying that I desired unfailing love and this Scripture not only resonated with me but quite frankly it provided me with a wakeup call I so desperately needed!

Who doesn't want to be loved? If you responded, "I don't," you are a liar. Sorry Sis, not my words but the Lord's. It's to our betterment to admit that we desire love, instead of denying it. Admit that you desire it and even mourn the fact that you don't have it, but please don't find yourself lying about your desire. We all want to be loved deeply for exactly who we are—regardless of our flaws. We want to be accepted and understood. Bottom line is, we want unconditional love; we crave it and thrive better when it is received. Now, the problem many of us face is when we try to receive this unfailing love from fallible human beings or worldly things.

The word "unfailing" used here in the Hebrew is anekleiptos, which means, "not left behind; describing what will not give out or cease." In another translation, the word used is "steadfast," which in the Hebrew is *emunah*, simply meaning, "firmness, faithfulness, and fidelity."

Be honest and examine those definitions; can any human being really live up to those standards? This fact remains, God is the ONLY One who can provide the type of never-ceasing love, consistency, and total acceptance we pant after.

I needed to sure myself up in the love of the Lord and learn to recite specific Bible verses. One being Psalm 63:3, "Because your love is better than life, my lips will glorify you." Or how about Jeremiah 31:3, "The LORD appeared to us in the past, saying: 'I have loved you with an everlasting love; I have drawn you with unfailing kindness'"?

This is what we long for: that crazy, relentless, unconditional, everlasting, knows-no-bounds type of love. Admit that you need this type of love and be bold to ask the Creator to allow you to experience what is already yours as a believer in Jesus Christ our Lord.

Prayer

Father God, thank You for Your love that is better than life itself! You are more than enough to me and I want to not only know this truth intellectually but feel it deep within the recesses of my heart. Lavish Your love on me so that I am not longing for approval or acceptance elsewhere. Help me to recognize that the unconditional, unyielding, undying love that I long for, lies in Your arms. Thank You Jesus,

It is in Your Name that I pray, Amen!

Today's Weapons

Ephesians 3:17b-18, NASB

_____

_____

_____

_____

Psalm 136:26

_____

_____

_____

_____

Romans 5:8

_____

_____

_____

_____

Your Turn

If you are single, in a loveless marriage, longing for friends and family to love you, well—find the love you desperately long for and need, in God. Do not diminish your desire for love from these people but realize He is the only One who can heal your heart and fill you with the unconditional love you crave. Write a love letter to your Heavenly Father today. Pour out your heart to Him and watch and listen to the ways in which He will respond.

_____

_____

_____

_____

_____

_____

_____

_____

_____

_____

_____

_____

_____

_____

_____

_____

_____

_____

_____

_____

_____

_____

Day 8
He Is With You

When you pass through the waters, I will be
with you; And through the rivers, they will not
overwhelm you. When you walk through fire, you
will not be scorched, Nor will the flame burn you."

— ISAIAH 43:2

O ne afternoon, I recall entering the room as my mom was watching a program about people who had experienced supernatural rescues from death. Do not ask me why, but my mother has a thing for the paranormal and all things supernatural. I almost wrote the show off as another "corny spooky show" until a certain story grabbed my undivided attention.

A woman appeared on the screen and began to recount the story of when she and her family were lost at sea with no sign of rescue. They had been fishing on a family vacation when a rip current came crashing through, sending their boat upside down as their bodies flew in different directions. Through tears, she explained how she prayed and cried out to God to "supernaturally save" her family. All looked lost as she found herself alone for minutes which felt like hours, frantically yelling each of her family members' names with trembling lips.

Just as she was about to give up, she saw her husband and son in the distance and thought, "Praise God," but then her attention quickly zeroed in on her missing daughter. After looking together for an hour, they could not find her and began to dread the impending outcome. Yet, they continued to pray and believe God for a miracle. Moments later a man appeared from "out of the blue" with their daughter as they swam back to shore.

Their daughter was resuscitated and appeared to be in good health. The mother explained how much she needed to thank the mystery man—but she never saw him again.

Upon returning home, the family attended a church service. Their pastor read his text for the sermon and there it was, Isaiah 43:2. The family wept as they recalled the events of the weekend and the marvelous truth this verse had become to them. I vividly remember her statement of how awesome God is that He would give them "their very own verse" to show that He loves them and is without a doubt always with them.

When I read Isaiah 43:2, I find it to be both a comforting and scary promise. God does not say, "I will keep you from the rivers or I will put out the flame before it becomes a blazing fire." No, Sis, He allows us to feel the water on our skin, even ingest a few gulps as we try to keep our head above the water.

He allows the flames to spread as if He kindled the fire Himself. However, the shouting point is that through it all He is with us and these elements that are known for wreaking havoc and creating natural disasters are no match for the Creator. Rest in these truths today as you face your individual river or fire.

I pray this story encourages you to believe that God can do the impossible and He is always with you! Never give up, even when all literally looks lost. God hears your cries and saves those who cry out to Him with a heart of integrity.

Prayer

God, my God, thank You for Your written Word that God, help me to remember that even when I don't feel Your presence, I know beyond a shadow of a doubt that You are with me. No situation is lost when I am the child of a God who can do anything but fail. Your Word declares that nothing is too hard for You and I choose to believe You. Remind me not to look at my present circumstances but instead to fix my eyes on You.

In Jesus name, Amen.

Today's Weapons

2 Corinthians 12:9, NIV

_____

_____

_____

_____

Ephesians 3:16, NIV

_____

_____

_____

_____

2 Chronicles 15:7, NIV

_____

_____

_____

_____

Your Turn

Think back on a time you literally thought you were not going to make it. How did God bring you out OR bring you through that trial? Get this picture in your mind of how God showed up and showed out and, hear me when I say, HE CAN DO IT AGAIN!

Never be fooled into thinking, this time is it, there is no way out, God will not be able to get me out of this one. That is a lie and I want you to cast it down in the name of Jesus!

Day 9
Trust God

"Trust in and rely confidently on the LORD
with all your heart. And do not rely on your own
insight or understanding. In all your ways know
and acknowledge and recognize Him,
And He will make your paths straight and smooth
[removing obstacles that block your way]."

— PROVERBS 3:5-6, AMP

"If you miss me, I will find you." The words one of my favorite female preachers shared with me that changed my life. I had won a contest where I was given the opportunity to speak with Heather Lindsey for 15 minutes! I remember telling her how afraid I was of missing the mark and totally getting God's will for my life all the way wrong.

I told her all about the paralyzing fear I experienced when thinking about making decisions for my future and just feeling so unsure of myself. She shared that she too suffered from those same fears and uncertainty, but one day God said, "Heather if you miss me, I will find you."

I'm passing those words on to you. Whatever you're unsure of, losing sleep over at night, becoming too afraid to step out in faith about, constantly "waiting to hear from the Lord" over... I beg you to please stop! Proverbs 3:5-6 is a widely popular passage of Scripture. Yet, how many of us blood-washed believers abide by this command: "Trust and rely confidently on the Lord with all your heart"? To dedicate ALL your heart to someone would mean that there is no room in your heart for fear, anxiety, worry, and doubt.

Recently, I was thinking about all the things I place blind trust in without giving it a second thought. I do not worry about Chick-fil-a running out of chicken when I have a craving for some well-done nuggets with Polynesian and Chick-fil-a sauce on the side.

I do not become anxious hoping and praying the water will come on when I go to brush my teeth in the morning. I do not fret when I am about to walk into a store with automatic doors, wondering if they will open for me as they did for the hundreds of other shoppers. I trust that my needs will be met. Why don't we adopt this same posture with the One who created us and promises to direct our paths when we acknowledge Him and do not lean on our own understanding? Might I suggest we stop worrying and trust in Him and His ability to lead us.

Now let me be abundantly clear, what I am not advocating is haphazardness; making decisions without consulting God but what I am saying is that you will make mistakes at times, get a few things wrong, but He will never let you fall (Psalm 37:24).

As a believer, the Spirit of God lives inside of you and will faithfully guide you into the will of God for your life as well as intercede on your behalf when you do not know what you should be praying for (John 16:13; Romans 8:26-27).

I trust and believe God for you and your concerns right now as you read this very sentence. He is for you and never against you, you need not worry when you have the Creator of the universe on your side. Wherever this finds you, do not harden your heart to God's truths. Soak them up, declare them aloud even if momentarily you only believe with your intellect and not your heart. Trust Him.

Prayer

God, my God, thank You for Your written Word that Dear Lord, I just want to say thank You for the reassurance that You will direct every one of my steps and that even when I take a wrong turn, You will be there to lovingly guide me back to You. Help me to never become too concerned with what Your will is, that I stay stuck and leave this world with a bunch of "woulda coulda shouldas" and one talent in the ground (Matthew 25:18). I am forever grateful to know that You search my heart and know the sincerity of its cry to do only Your good, pleasing, and perfect will.

In Jesus name, Amen.

Today's Weapons

Psalm 37:23

_____

_____

_____

_____

Isaiah 30:21

_____

_____

_____

_____

Psalm 32:8

_____

_____

_____

_____

Your Turn

If there is one thing I have learned throughout my journey with God, it is this: Don't ever think your desire to be led by God is greater than His desire to lead you. We are His people, called by His Name!

Think about that for a minute. Why do you doubt that He will give you clear directions to carry out His will for your life that will bring Him glory? With that being said, what decision, business venture, relationship, etc. have you been agonizing over and afraid of missing God's will for your life if you actually followed through?

What excuses have you used to enable you to stall and continue in your spiritual paralysis? I challenge you to create **3 actions steps** that you can carry out within the next 3 weeks (a step a week) that will get you closer to whatever God has called you to do. Do not overthink it, they can be small things but make them specific, realistic, obtainable, and observable.

Day 10
Faith In Action

"Thus also faith by itself,
if it does not have works, is dead."

— JAMES 2:17, NKJV

"**O**uch!" I said silently to myself, experiencing intense pain in my left knee while in church. I'm a tall girl and I had to sit in the balcony which is lower body suicide for anyone over 5'5. But for me, my knee pain began about 4 months earlier when I decided to do a home kickboxing workout. I went to perform a combo complete with a kick, uppercut, and right hook and well... let's just say something went terribly wrong.

I waited quite a while to get it checked out by the doctor (I know, I know, not good) and when I did, I was sure something was definitely "not right." However, I found that I had a bad case of "runner's knee" and, as the doc explained it, my knee was not sitting comfortably in the groove of the socket and that was the source of the pain. She recommended I do exercises daily, and my prognosis looked pretty good. So, I guess this is where I admit that I did not practice every day like I should have. I always had excuses, some reason as to why something else I was doing took precedence over my ailing knee.

James is a hard-hitting book in the Bible. Theologians believe James was Jesus' half-brother who did not believe in Jesus until after His death. James became a believer and rose to be a prominent leader in the Jerusalem church. James was loving in his speech as evidenced by the constant familial greeting of "brother and sister" to the first century Jewish Christians. Yet, James was also firm and direct.

In our passage today, he calls out those who claim to love God and have faith, but their actions indicate otherwise. James called them out for praying for those in need instead of being a conduit to meet their needs.

He essentially said to the people: Faith-filled prayers devoid of action is no faith at all.

As I sat in church after a month of not exercising habitually as I should have, I had a strong sense that God was saying, "Why are you expecting healing without any work, diligence, or consistency?" After I got over the shock of being "read" by the Lord, I sat and pondered how true His words were and how they extended beyond the physical to the spiritual realm.

How many times have you and I become frustrated with what we perceive as a lack of healing or breakthrough?

But if we honestly take a self-inventory, we put in relatively little effort to "join with God," if you will, to cause any results to swing in our favor. You know like when people claim they don't "hear from God" but they have a non-existent prayer life, or when others say they want to know God better but they rarely read His Word, or those who are experiencing turmoil in their marriages but won't even think about forgiving their spouse. Or let me put it back on myself; when I ask for more faith and courage, but I never put myself in positions where I need to simply rely on God and stretch those "faith muscles."

I think it is safe to say we have all been guilty of trying to "get something for nothing." Well God is saying to you and me, "No more!" It's time to start working for what we desire and not simply hoping and praying they will come to pass.

Prayer

God, my God, thank You for Your written Word that Lord, I come before Your throne with a humble heart of repentance. Forgive me for my laziness, my fear, and my complacency. Thank You for reminding me that I must not simply desire for things to happen but that I also need to be active in my healing. Lord help me to always do what I can before You do
the rest.

In Jesus name, Amen.

Today's Weapons

Matthew 9:20-21, KJV

_____

_____

_____

_____

Matthew 9:2, NIV

_____

_____

_____

_____

1 Kings 17:15-16, NIV

_____

_____

_____

_____

Your Turn

Sis, I love you and I am not going to mince words here: Whatever you know beyond a shadow of a doubt you need to be doing, do it! Did God tell you to write a business plan, a book, quit a job, start exercising more, pray more, forgive someone, or join a ministry?

You must be obedient. God will meet you at your level of faith! Those things will not take care of themselves but once you tackle them, God WILL take care of you!

_____

_____

_____

_____

_____

_____

_____

_____

_____

_____

_____

_____

_____

_____

_____

_____

_____

_____

_____

_____

_____

_____

_____

Day 11
Love In Action

"Above all, love each other deeply,
because love covers over a multitude of sins."

— 1 PETER 4:8

Oddly enough, reading this verse reminds me of makeup. For months now, I have noticed bumps pop up like uninvited guests and leave nasty little scars as their going away present. I searched YouTube and, to my surprise, found people suffering from far more severe scarring than me. However, no one would ever know it once they painted over their scars using a few good techniques and some trusted makeup products. Whatever these women used was just enough to conceal even the nastiest and problematic areas on their skin.

This, my friend, is what we, as blood- washed believers, radiating with the love of God are supposed to be for those whose sin we encounter. We are to be their "spiritual makeup" if you will. Most of us, however, have a hard time "covering" sins because we are not allowing God to fill us with the love required to do so.

The word *cover* here refers to the Greek word *kalupto*, which means "to veil, hide, conceal, envelop; to pardon them." If any of us are going to properly conceal, envelop, and pardon the sin of others against us, we must rely on the power of God. In keeping with the makeup analogy, God must be the foundation, concealer, and every other product one can think of, while we are to be His brushes. At times, many of us believe we love well; that is until we are face-to-face with people's brokenness and worst scars. This is when we experience the difficulty of letting go of the disappointment and pain without simultaneously letting go of the perpetrator of the offense in the process.

The results of such instances are treacherous; ranging from residual anger, bitterness, and contention, to refusing to allow yourself to be vulnerable with anyone else again.

God's love, however, commands us to love in such a way that there is no room for those feelings of strife to reside within. When you and I grasp that the true and living God Himself, who is love, is living on the inside of us, love undergoes its transformation from a noun to a verb.

To love each other well looks like being patient, kind, never envying, never boasting, resisting pride, seeking to honor, never seeking to exalt self, not easily angered, keeping no record of wrongs, scorning evil and delighting in the truth, protecting, trusting, hoping, and never failing (1 Corinthians 13:4-7). This is the perfect love that drives out the fear of being sinned against again. How? Because you are filled with God who enables you to continue to cover a multitude of sins because of His love!

Prayer

God, my God, thank You for Your written Word that Lord, I come before Your throne with a humble heart of repentance. Forgive me for my laziness, my fear, and my complacency. Thank You for reminding me that I must not simply desire for things to happen but that I also need to be active in my healing. Lord help me to always do what I can before You do
the rest.

In Jesus name, Amen.

Today's Weapons

1 Corinthians 13:4-7, NIV

_____
_____
_____
_____

Ephesians 4:2, NLT

_____
_____
_____
_____

Colossians 3:13, NIV

_____
_____
_____
_____

Your Turn

Is there someone on your mind right now that you know you have not forgiven? Maybe you believe they have committed the ultimate sin or sins against you, and your love simply cannot cover their grievous behavior. It is safe to say, you are right.

Your love cannot cover that type of sin... but God's can. Meditate on the Scriptures today and ask God to infuse you with so much of His love, you can use it to cover the multitude of sins you have experienced at the hands of another. Be the brush that God can use to accomplish His will that we love one another well; this will not be easy, but you do not have to do it alone.

Day 12
Stay Planted

"For we walk by faith, not by sight."
— 2 CORINTHIANS 5:7

One night I went to bed with such a heavy heart. I felt so defeated, insecure, and lost. I felt like I was miles away from God and that He had stopped speaking to me—like I was in a spiritual desert. I ruminated over the trajectory of my life and concluded that nothing that I was doing was working. I was stuck in a miserable job, no man, and no plan in sight to reach my dreams I believed He placed on the inside of me. After my pity party, I decided to pray and go to bed.

At three a.m., the Holy Spirit reminded of the first Psalm I ever memorized, Psalm 1:1-3, "Blessed is the one who does not walk in step with the wicked or stand in the way that sinners take or sit in the company of mockers, but whose delight is in the law of the Lord, and who meditates on his law day and night. That person is like a tree planted by the streams of water, which yields its fruit in season and whose leaf does not wither— whatever they do prospers."

The Lord literally whispered, "Stay planted" or at least that is the impression I felt on my mind and heart. I had to truly look at the Psalm and see that it tells us to be like a tree planted by the river which yields its fruit in due season. If things are not happening right now it is not grounds for you to move, stay planted next to your water source. The frustration you are experiencing is simply because you are out of season.

I beg you to stay rooted and meditate on the Word so God can water the seeds of your heart. Your due season is contingent upon your ability to stay planted despite what you see.

I believe that God is telling you, just like He told me, to stay planted. Keep on reading His Word day and night, keep on being mindful of those you surround yourself with—and that fruit is coming; the season of harvest is coming but in due time not your timing. Your leaf will not wither and die and whatever you do for Him, whether big or small, will prosper.

Prayer

God, my God, thank You for Your written Word that God, I need You to provide me with the water I need to survive in this season of my life. Help me to hold tight to Your Word and believe that in due season I will see the fruit that I have been planting. Thank You for keeping me.

In Jesus name, Amen!

Today's Weapons

Galatians 6:9, NLT

_____

_____

_____

_____

James 4:10, NIV

_____

_____

_____

_____

Isaiah 30: 18-19, NIV

_____

_____

_____

_____

Your Turn

I challenge you to read Psalm 1:1-3 and ask yourself if you are living like the person described in it, and if you are not, ask God what you need to do to become this person who is indeed BLESSED.

_____

_____

_____

_____

_____

_____

_____

_____

_____

_____

_____

_____

_____

_____

Day 13
Wisdom Yields Patience

"A person's wisdom yields patience;
it is to one's glory to overlook an offense"

— PROVERBS 19:11

D o you find yourself easily offended? Are you hyper-sensitive to perceived slights; waiting on edge at the possibility of what someone will say and or do to hurt you? If you answered yes, you are not alone! I will admit that God has been pruning me in this area, so I am A LOT better than I used to be... but it is still a struggle.

Wisdom yields patience—I think this is an interesting statement that warrants exploration. Where does wisdom come from? Well, my Bible tells me that it comes from God (Proverbs 9:10; James 1:5).

Essentially, you and I take the offense to God and He will give us patience. I am not sure how many times I have gone to God in prayer, with the intention of "tittle-tattling" on someone, and He has softened my stony heart by showing me secrets of sins and strongholds that person was struggling with. The revelation and knowledge from God enabled me to gain a new-found tolerance for my offender because with insight comes patience.

I am reminded of the saying: "When you know better, you do better." God helps me to know better when I take the offense to Him and get the inside scoop on the situation. But, just like anything else in life, to whom much is given, much is required. With the wisdom I acquire from the Lord, I am expected to respond accordingly, and subsequently release the other party of the debt I believe they owe.

I will never forget the day God showed me this truth by infusing me with patience, strength, grace, and humility to lovingly respond to an offender because I was made aware of the state of the heart from whence the offense came.

Just for a second, I want you to ponder one of God's greatest attributes—His long-suffering. He is in the know about everyone and everything, yet He is still patient. Not merely patient, but He is also gracious and ready and willing to forgive when confession and repentance are brought to His throne.

To reach a point where you and I are also patient and gracious despite a person's actions, we must seek wisdom to grasp things from God's perspective. This brings us to the point of glory which is really God being glorified due to the work He's doing in and through us. God is on full display in our lives when we forgive quickly; when we put our pride to the side and practice patience and extend mercy to those around us.

Prayer

God, my God, thank You for Your written Word that Lord, you know how easily I can become offended and get the "cut-you-off spirit." Help me to guard against this ugly defense mechanism and view Your people the way that You do. Guide my words, soften my heart, and help me to extend my hand in forgiveness.

In Jesus name, Amen.

Today's Weapons

Matthew 5:9, NIV

_____

_____

_____

_____

Romans 3:23, NIV

_____

_____

_____

_____

James 2:13, NIV

_____

_____

_____

_____

Your Turn

Sis, you already know what I am about to say... who is on your heart and mind as you read today's devo? Who is it that offends you the most? Have you taken the situation before God? Have you sought His wisdom on the matter? If your answer is no, my strong suggestion is that you go before the Throne of Grace and ask God to show you how to relate to that person or those persons. Being easily offended is like being locked in a prison that you have the keys to—it is a choice. Please make the choice today to set yourself free.

Day 14
When God Changes Your Plans

"The heart of man plans his way,
but the LORD establishes his steps."

— PROVERBS 16:9, ESV

"God must love others more than He loves me. He never seems to answer my prayer requests... or at least not the way I send them up. It seems like everything I plan for and desire gets flipped, turned upside down." Painful words to type, but this had sadly become my juvenile mindset when I failed to consider this powerful truth: "But the LORD establishes my steps."

Have you ever wanted something realllllyyyy (you read that right, extra l's and y's to emphasize my point!) bad? I mean you planned for it, worked hard at it, prayed for it, and honestly believed God that it would happen... only to have things go in the opposite direction. You cannot see me, but I am waving one hand in the air, screaming, "Sis, I have!" Between you and me, I have a bad habit of holding fast to rigid ideals and what "should be and will be" if I do "x, y, and z." Inevitably, God had to show me the hard way that I can plan "till the cows come home" but He would ultimately be the deciding factor in which paths my feet will take.

The word establishes in this text means determines, prepares, provides, directs, or firmly roots, and decides. An example of this would be developing a rough draft—your ideas, your plans, your hearts desires... and then handing your work over to your boss or editor for review. They ultimately have the final say on what stays and what goes.

This is the same with God, but He is not simply an editor, but a Divine Creator and a good, good Father who changes our plans because He has something better in mind.

God's plans for our lives are always superior to ours because He does things from an eternal perspective, knowing the end from the beginning.

So, the next time your plans are derailed—the interviewer for the potential new job suddenly stops calling, the sale on your dream home falls through, the love of your life decides the relationship just isn't working for them anymore, or whatever else you carefully planned out begins to fall apart—remember that God is sovereign, and He is directing your path because He knows a better way. Let us learn to trust Him.

Prayer

God, my God, thank You for Your written Word that Lord, I admit that there are times where I pridefully think I know what is best for my life. Please forgive my arrogance and show me the way everlasting. Lead my feet on level ground and show me the best pathway to take. I know Your plans for my life will blow my mind and remind me that You can do exceedingly above and beyond what I could ever ask or imagine.

In Jesus name, Amen.

Today's Weapons

Proverbs 16:3, NIV

_____
_____
_____
_____

Ephesians 2:10, NLT

_____
_____
_____
_____

Psalm 32:8, NLT

_____
_____
_____
_____

Your Turn

Has God ever changed your plans? Have you been honest about your thoughts and feelings regarding this change or changes that He has sovereignly made?

If you have not done so, go before God and cast your cares upon Him because He cares for you. Be honest in your hurt, pain, confusion, and even anger for what you thought would be, but ultimately is not your reality. Ask Him to provide you with peace to accept His perfect will for your life.

Day 15
Let It Go

"Cease striving and know that I am God;
I will be exalted among the nations,
I will be exalted in the earth."

— PSALM 46:10, NASB

"Let it go." These three words spoken by the Holy Spirit to my heart, rocked me as I wept in prayer. Through sobs, I remember saying, "But, how can I God? Why should I let them get off without giving them a piece of my mind? If You want me to do this, I need Your help."

The short story is someone I love had said and done some things that left me feeling dishonored, disrespected, and disregarded. I wanted to forgive, I really wanted to... but not without saying my piece.

I needed to make them feel the weight and the magnitude of what they had done. I wanted to see their face as I attempted to speak the truth in love and call them out on their sinful behavior, but truth be told, all I really wanted to do was take vengeance into my own hands. I became obsessive, ferociously writing notes on my phone of what I would say, which Scriptures I would quote to support my claims, ruminating on the situation and playing the conversation in my head over and over again—switching their response and then mine, and then theirs again, and then mine. It was pure insanity!

I knew it had to stop and that is when my knees hit the floor and I begged God to help me forgive and, "Get over this, once and for all!" I was so tired, and that is when I heard it, "Let it go." After my teary rebuttals, I realized exactly what the Lord wanted me to do... surrender and assure myself that He is God.

Instantly, Psalm 46:10, which in other versions may read, "Be still, and know that I am God" or "Stop your fighting—and know that I am God" appeared in my head as if it were in neon lights.

That day in my room, I had to decide to acquiesce to the full power and protection of Almighty God. In my surrender, He would be lifted up. He would be known among nations and all the earth because it is only when God does the fighting that He can be glorified. You and I can do nothing in our own volition and in our own power, and expect God to be made manifest and justice be served. No, my friend, He must do what only He can do, and He must know that you acknowledge this truth.

Prayer

Father God, thank You! Thank You for Your gentle whispers that stop me in my tracks and lovingly demand that I remember who You are in my life. Help me to never forget that You fight for me and You will ultimately have the final say in any situation. Things may seem unfair, unjust, and downright unfixable but You are a just, holy, and righteous God that will make all things right in Your timing.

In Jesus name I pray, Amen.

Today's Weapons

Exodus 14:14, NIV

_____

_____

_____

_____

Romans 12:19, NIV

_____

_____

_____

_____

Joshua 23:10-11, NIV

_____

_____

_____

_____

Your Turn

I will not beat around the bush here. As you read today's devo, who or what was on your mind? What is the Lord commanding you to let go of? Talk to Him about it and take the necessary steps to be obedient, you are not alone.

_____

_____

_____

_____

_____

_____

_____

_____

_____

_____

_____

_____

_____

Day 16
Love As He Loved

"We love because he first loved us.
Whoever claims to love God yet hates a brother
or sister is a liar. For whoever does not love their
brother or sister, whom they have seen,
cannot love God, whom they have not seen."

— 1 JOHN 4:19-20, NIV

Instant conviction is what most of us feel when we read those verses. I recall the day I was scrolling down my Instagram feed and a certain person's name popped up and, do not judge me, but I instantly rolled my eyes and felt a tightness in my face and chest. I was not trying to see anything they had to say. To make matters worse, a few weeks before I found myself angry at the grace this person was receiving because, quite frankly, I believed they did not deserve any.

During this time, my church was reading through the book of Jonah, a book I just so happened to be studying for weeks before my church embarked upon this journey. "You are having a Jonah moment," is what I heard the Holy Spirit say or shall I say impress upon my mind and heart. It alarmed me, and I wanted to deny such an accusation, not Jonah! ... But it was true. I had no love, mercy, grace, or relent for this person, a fellow believer in the faith.

Nothing tests a believer quite like a difficult brother or sister in the faith. Maybe a boss, family member, fellow ministry leader, co-worker, or neighbor has been the source of your anger, frustration, or even hate. Perhaps, you have tried to rationalize your behavior toward them because they are self-serving, rude, needy, prideful or any other sinful trait you can use to fill in the blank to describe them.

However, God simply does not care what they have done or may continue to do; as far as He is concerned, you, me, we, must love them! Our beloved example, Jesus commands us to love one another as He loved us. This display of love is how we will be identifiable to everyone—the believer and unbeliever alike.

Will this be hard? Will it be painful? Will you want to quit? Yes, yes, and yes. But your love for those who you deem downright unlovable and do not love you back, sets you apart from those of the world. Jesus reminded the disciples: "If you love those who love you, what credit is that to you? Even sinners love those who love them" (Luke 6:32). This is what I call a major "gut check." You and I are not doing anyone any favors by loving those who love us or being kind to those who are kind to us. No, Sis, the true test of being a disciple of Christ and loving like Him, means being graceful and merciful to those who hate, annoy, dishonor, slander, and degrade us. It is when we do this that we can be called "children of the Most High" (Luke 6:35) and actually live up to that name.

Prayer

Dear Lord, forgive me for my cold, unrelenting, and calloused heart toward people who I think are difficult and hard to love. I need Your help to love how You command me to love. I simply cannot do this in my own strength. Help me to see people the way You see them. Fill me with Your grace and mercy that extends to even the most difficult brother and sister in the faith. Bind my heart with Your unity, peace, humility, and forgiveness. I ask these things in your name.

In Jesus name I pray, Amen.

Today's Weapons

Luke 6:32

_____

_____

_____

_____

Luke 6:35

_____

_____

_____

_____

Jonah 4:2

_____

_____

_____

_____

Your Turn

I was so deeply impacted by my study of the book of Jonah that I want you to share in that goodness. Today, read the book of Jonah (it is only four chapters) and meditate on the Lord's compassion for a people who simply did not deserve it.

Sis, you and I are a part of "those people," yet the Lord is gracious and compassionate. Let these words wash over you and ask the Lord to help you have mercy and love for even the most undeserving and sinful people. Refuse to have a "Jonah moment" and allow the Lord to work in your heart. Record your thoughts below.

Day 17
He's Guiding You

But blessed is the one who trusts in the Lord,
whose confidence is in him."
— JEREMIAH 17:7, NIV

"O h no!!" My reaction as my phone fell from the console into the cracks of my passenger seat. "Great, how am I ever supposed to see how to get where I am going?" I was late driving to a client's home that I had visited a few times before but the normal route I'd taken each time was blocked off! If you are anything like me or the other millions, possibly billions of people who use our smartphones' GPS to magically guide us to our destinations, you can only imagine the frustration and the fear I was experiencing in that moment.

I remember continuing straight ahead and praying I'd find my way; some way, somehow and then I heard it, it was faint, and I had to turn the radio down to cancel every distraction and interference but there it was: "In 2.5 miles turn left."

My heart rate slowly started to return to normal, yet all the while I really wished I could SEE my GPS. I was oh so thankful to hear it guiding me but that was not enough... no, I wanted to have my device in my hand, glance at it, look at the ETA, and the red lines showing detours up ahead. I needed to make sure I could trust the directions I was being given. Bottom line is, I wanted control and yielding to that still small voice coming from under my seat just in time for me to turn here or there was not cutting it for me. I wanted familiarity. I craved comfort. Do you see where I am going with this? Can you relate?

Our text for today is found in the book of Jeremiah, who many affectionately refer to as, "The Weeping Prophet."

Jeremiah wept because God told him to prophesy of the impending judgment that would come upon Israel due to their habitual sin and disobedience.

Verse 7 is couched between the persistent sin of Judah and the deceitful heart of man. God outlined curses and blessings due to very specific behaviors: trust in man versus trust in God

God commanded Jeremiah to tell the people that placing trust in your own wisdom and the strength of man only turns your heart from God. In fact, God says this type of person is so disillusioned they lack the ability to discern when good is in front of them. Instead, the person who places their trust in mankind becomes paralyzed in infertile places yet expects seeds to sprout up and grow. But the one who actively decides to place trust in the Lord, no matter what may be occurring in the atmosphere, is guaranteed blessing.

The verse is too good not to share: "They will be like a tree planted by the water that sends out its roots by the stream. It does not fear when heat comes; its leaves are always green. It has no worries in a year of drought and never fails to bear fruit" (17:8). "No worries in the year of drought" is what I believe we are all desiring. No fear or anxiety when things seem out of our control because we simply trust in the Lord who we cannot see or maybe even hear clearly at times, but we can trust Him at His Word.

Even now, I cannot help but chuckle at how God could show me a spiritual picture of my relationship with Him through such a mundane occurrence as my cellphone dropping out of my reach. I was trusting in my own understanding that day, panicking because I could not see who was guiding me and God reminded me that this is much like my disposition with Him when life gets tricky. But the truth is, even when we can't see Him, He's guiding us.

Sis, how many times have you and I lost it when God seems to drop below the passenger seat and is seemingly out of our sight and reach? Most of us experienced God's voice very clearly, loud even, when we were first adopted into the family of God through Christ. However, I can attest to God's voice becoming faint and even what I call "radio silent" as I have grown in Him. What is that all about? I believe it is because He desires for you and me to trust Him. He is longing for the day when one-step directions that seem scary and confusing, remain no match for our love for Him, and therefore, we practice OBEDIENCE and we demonstrate TRUST. Is that day today?

Prayer

Dear God, forgive me for allowing fear and doubt to cause me to question if You are with me when things seem uncertain and unfamiliar. Lord allow me to listen intently for Your loving guidance even when it does not come as I think it ought. Lord give me the courage I need to not only listen to your voice but to then act in obedience even if I tremble every step of the way. Draw me closer to you in and out of season.

In Jesus Name, Amen.

Today's Weapons

Psalm 9:10

_____

_____

_____

_____

Psalm 56:3

_____

_____

_____

_____

Proverbs 28:26

_____

_____

_____

_____

Your Turn

How many times do you struggle to follow through in obedience because it doesn't look right to you, you don't know the route, the road is less traveled and unpopular, the directions are unfamiliar? If you are like me, you may think, "These directions are being given one at a time, and I need a list I can scroll through and know where I'm going before I'm 500 ft. away." Sis, I encourage you to do a "heart check" right now.

Can God count on you to keep going even when you can't hear Him as loud or as frequently as you would like? Can He count on your obedience before your understanding? Remember, delayed obedience is still disobedience in the eyes of God. Record your answers to these questions and go before the Lord in prayer.

Day 18
Even If He Doesn't

"But even if he does not, we want you to know,
Your Majesty, that we will not serve your gods
or worship the image of gold you have set up.

— DANIEL 3:18

Even if He doesn't... those words had been ringing in my head over the course of a few weeks. I led life group and I remember hastily rummaging through my tattered journal to reference this verse in Daniel that I had been studying. I boldly stated, "I have decided to get an 'even if He doesn't,' in my spirit!" I was fired up and talking about my declaration to serve God even if my deepest desires go unrealized in this lifetime on this side of Heaven.

A month later, the Associate Pastor of my church gets up for the doxology and tearfully speaks of this same verse in Daniel 3. He prayed that the collective body would bend but never break, cry but never cease to honor God with the fruit of the lips, question but never quit, and sorrow but never surrender or succumb to the lies of the enemy. I cried my eyes out that morning because I could not help but think about all my friends and family who desired noble things like healing, a job, godly friendships, and more. Friends and family who were faithfully prepared to serve God even if He never provided.

My own pastor and his wife had been praying for healing as his wife had battled with cancer six times, was the recipient of a liver transplant 10 years ago, and yet found themselves praying she would be bumped up on the list for another as her body rejected the miracle she received years before.

Not to mention the things I desired: healing in my body, restored relationships, salvation for my family and friends, a godly marriage, children, a home, and the list goes on.

But in that moment, none of those unmet desires could hold a candle to the unwavering love and the resolve I have to serve a God who has the power to change my circumstances but may see fit in His infinite wisdom to leave them as they are.

If you are unfamiliar with this passage, the three Hebrew boys, Shadrach, Meshach, and Abednego were chosen along with Daniel by King Nebuchadnezzar's chief official to serve the king. To be chosen, the requirements were that they were young, without physical defect, handsome, well informed, quick to understand, and qualified to serve in the king's place (Daniel 1:4a).

These young fine men of God had it going on! But they were not chosen for some great purpose, no they were chosen to serve a selfish king who had besieged their home of Jerusalem and ordered them exiled to Babylon.

In Babylon, they (along with Daniel) quickly rose to ranks because of their character and the hand of God upon their lives. Daniel, who the king was especially fond of after he interpreted a vexing dream, found himself ruler over the entire province of Babylon and the king honored Daniel's request to place Shadrach, Meshach, and Abednego as administrators over the province of Babylon.

Picture it, these noble young men were thriving in a foreign land and receiving favor from a king who did not know God. Yet, when faced with a decision as to whether to bow down to the image of gold the king had resurrected or risk death and serve the only true and living God, they chose the latter.

They not only chose the latter, but they boldly professed: "If we are thrown into the blazing furnace, the God we serve is able to deliver us from it, and he will deliver us from Your Majesty's hand. But even if he does not, we want you to know, Your Majesty, that we will not serve your gods or worship the image of gold you have set up" (Daniel 3:17-18).

They attested to the Lord's sovereignty and power and acknowledged that even if He did not do what they knew the Lord to be more than capable of doing, they would still serve Him and Him alone. Can you say the same?

Prayer

Lord, I know You declare, "As the heavens are higher than the earth, so are my ways higher than your ways and my thoughts than your thoughts" (Isaiah 55:9). But sometimes it still hurts when I do not understand why You are allowing my life to unfold as it is. Yet, I will trust You! Even though my flesh and my heart may fail, God, You are the strength of my heart and my portion forever" (Psalm 73:26). I will serve You. Help me to cling to You in every season of my life.

In Jesus name, Amen.

Today's Weapons

Leviticus 19:4

_____

_____

_____

_____

Joshua 24:15

_____

_____

_____

_____

Acts 5:29-32

_____

_____

_____

_____

Your Turn

I do not know about you, but todays devo hits home for me. If you haven't already read the story of the three Hebrew boys, spoiler alert... God came through! However, that is not always the story of every believer trusting God for a miracle. At this very moment, I type with godly desires wedged deep in my heart yet unfulfilled. I live every day in the tension of both the peace and pain of knowing nothing is too hard for God and that He can change my situation whenever He pleases but for now it remains the same.

With that being said, the question I am about to ask you to ponder comes from someone who knows what you are going through. Will you serve God with all your heart, soul, strength, and all your mind... even if He does not do _____. Put your "it" in the space or your "it's."

Be transparent today about your desires, fears, frustrations, questions, and whatever else. Pledge today, to get an "even if He doesn't in your spirit," it will change your perspective and life!

_____

_____

_____

_____

_____

_____

_____

_____

_____

_____

_____

_____

_____

_____

_____

_____

_____

Day 19
Faith In Action

"They received help against these enemies
because they cried out to God in battle,
and the Hagrites and all their allies were handed
over to them. He was receptive to their prayer
because they trusted in him."

— 1 CHRONICLES 5:20, CSB

H ave you ever been at work and a task is just beyond your job description and/or your level of expertise, or perhaps simply above your paygrade, if we keep it real? If you have, you know all about drafting the email for your boss, explaining the situation and then kindly attaching two little words: "Please advise." I am sure you are more than competent, exceptional even, at whatever it is you do.

But let's face it, no matter how skilled we are, there will come a time when we will need assistance from someone who is higher and more accomplished than ourselves.

In today's text, we find 44,760 skillful, crafty, strong, and capable armed men of Reuben, Gad, and the half-tribe of Manasseh. These men could fight, I mean they were trained in combat, toting shields, swords, and bows that they were not afraid to use. Fighting is what they did for a living and they were darn good at it. However, one day in the middle of their battle against the Hagrites, the Tethurites, the Naphishites, and the Nodabites, the tribes of Reuben, and the rest of the gang, as skilled as they were, cried out to God for help.

They realized that even in all their God-given talent, ability, and strength they were about to lose this battle. The remarkable part about this story is God's faithfulness due to the display of His people's humility.

These grown men were not afraid to cry out in desperation to God in front of their adversaries. What's more, is that God responded to their prayers not only because of their humble-hearts posture but because they trusted in Him. Ahhh... there it is again, trust.

There is something about this small four-letter word that just makes the heart of God leap and releases His hand of blessings on behalf of those who place their trust in Him. These men could have trusted in their weapons of war, their intellect, experience, expertise, and numbers—yet they chose to trust in God, and it was a choice that was richly rewarded. They won the battle that day and the Bible states, "Many of the Hagrites were killed in the battle because God was fighting against them" (1 Chronicles 5:22).

Sometimes life is just outside our scope of understanding; too much for us to handle and we need some help, the kind of help that only the Lord Himself can provide.

We can all agree that sometimes it is hard to distinguish when we should stop fighting in our own strength. Calling on God is a tough call to make when we are skilled and similar problems have been conquered with our natural abilities. Let these warriors be an example of humility, honor, and hope. Humble yourself before God, honor Him above your own capabilities, and put your hope in Him to hear your cry for help and save you.

Prayer

Father God, today I humble myself under Your mighty hand and in due time You will lift me up in honor. I know that there are battles that I will never win in my own strength, so I look to You as the author and finisher of my faith to do what I could never do. I place my trust in You today and forevermore. This is not always easy when my human reasoning tries to tell me I know the better route or that I can do it on my own. Grant me the wisdom to know when You have, in fact, given me the strength and tools I need to accomplish victory and when I needed to cry out to You in the middle of the battle.

In Jesus Name I pray, Amen.

Today's Weapons

Ephesians 3:20

_____
_____
_____
_____

Psalm 37:23-24

_____
_____
_____
_____

Galatians 5:25

_____
_____
_____
_____

Your Turn

What is God speaking to you about today? Is there a battle you have been fighting on your own? What do you need to cry out to Him about today and trust that He will take care of in His infinite power and wisdom? Remember, "The Lord is near all who call out to him, all who call out to him with integrity. He fulfills the desires of those who fear him; he hears their cry for help and saves them" (Psalm 145:18-19). Will you ask Him to save you today?

Day 20
Expectations

"But Naaman was furious and went away and said, "Behold, I thought, 'He will surely come out to me and stand and call on the name of the LORD his God, and wave his hand over the place and cure the leper."

— 2 KINGS 5:11, NASB

P icture it, a war has broken out in your hometown and you have just been ripped away from your family; stolen from your own home by the enemy and taken to a foreign place to work indefinitely as a slave. Your master has an illness and you know someone back home who can surely cure his condition, are you going to speak up and be conduit to your master's healing or let him remain in bondage?

For many of you the answer is a resounding no! Maybe even a few of you read that and thought, "What kind of the question is that?" I promise I have not lost my marbles; this scenario is an intricate part of today's text.

Naaman, commander of the army of Aram was a mighty warrior but had a skin disease, most likely a form of leprosy. After raiding Israel, he brought back a young girl to serve his wife. When this young woman of God laid eyes on her master's condition, she immediately thought of a solution and told her mistress, Naaman's wife. The solution to Naaman's problem lay in the hands of the prophet Elisha who the servant girl was sure could heal Naaman.

Upon Naaman's entrance to Elisha's house, Elisha sent a messenger to give Naaman instructions for healing. At the sound of the instructions (v 10), Naaman was infuriated and walked away.

Naaman's reaction was based on three expectations or assumptions: 1. Elisha would surely personally come out to meet him; 2. He would call upon the Lord God of Israel for healing; 3. The healing process would be grand and interpersonal. Naaman almost missed out on healing and salvation (2 Kings 5:15) if it were not for his servants who talked him into carrying out Elisha's instructions (2 Kings 5:13).

At first glance, Naaman seems pompous and ungrateful. Was Naaman offended at the instruction to wash in the Jordan because it implied that he was unclean? We clearly see in the text that he thought the muddy Jordan river was too dirty and there were other rivers he could take a dive in that were much closer and convenient. How dare he?! Think about that poor sweet servant girl who stifled her pain and possible bitterness to tell her oppressors about Elisha in the first place. Naaman then has the nerve to get angry because the circumstances surrounding his healing did not go according to his plan.

However, before you get indignant, have you ever found yourself upset with God due to the way He chose to deliver you? Did His plan not go according to your expectations? Perhaps one of these scenarios is familiar to you:

"Surely He has something better planned for me? I have two degrees and I must settle for this position and accept this pay?"

OR

"I thought I was going to naturally birth multiple children, not foster and adopt to create our family."

OR

"I thought I was going to be the next one to get married. Why do I have to help plan and attend yet another friend's wedding?"

Whatever your situation may be, sometimes God's way of granting you the breakthrough, the healing, the deliverance that you so desperately need, looks way less grand and quite mundane in your own eyes.

Don't let your expectations block your breakthrough. Your ability to act in obedience regardless of how the instructions from God make you feel is what will stand in between you and your healing. Humility is what will enable your obedience. Do you, like Naaman, need to humble yourself today?

Prayer

God, my God, thank You for Your written Word that Dear Lord, it is extremely difficult to accept situations when they do not meet or exceed my expectations. Help me to trust that whichever way You deem fit to bring about my healing, is the only and best way that it could get done. Lord, I repent of pride and believing that I deserve something when I do not deserve anything that You so graciously provide me, including the gift of salvation through Your One and only Son, Jesus Christ. Open my eyes to see life from Your perspective.

In Jesus name, Amen.

Today's Weapons

John 4:48:

_____

_____

_____

_____

Proverbs 13:10:

_____

_____

_____

_____

John 6:66-69

_____

_____

_____

_____

Your Turn

Read Matthew 15:21-28. Take in the whole scene. What thoughts and feelings came up for you while reading? This story has been labeled by some as a controversial one. Many read it and think Jesus would not have dared call a woman a dog, would he? But verbiage aside, fix your attention on the Canaanite woman's posture, both her body and heart. She drops to her knees in reverence even after Jesus tells her he came for Israel, not the Gentiles. She stays that way and continues to ask for crumbs after Jesus says, "It is not right to take the children's bread and toss it to the dogs."

She continues with tenacity and says she will eat the crumbs left behind from their meal. Sis, you and I are like that Gentile woman, undeserving of anything from God but by our faith in Jesus we are brought into the family of God and made whole.

Pay close attention to the Canaanite's woman's actions and words. Jesus seems to outright refuse her request for help, yet she does not budge. What stands out to you? Name some of the attributes she displays in this story. How does her faith encourage you to keep seeking God even when your expectations are not met in His responses?

_____

_____

_____

_____

_____

_____

_____

_____

_____

_____

_____

_____

_____

_____

_____

Day 21
Love Begets Love

Therefore I say to you, her sins, which are many,
are forgiven, for she loved much;
but he who is forgiven little, loves little."

— LUKE 7:47, AMP

G rowing up, I remember my great-grandmother would always hire handymen or women for odd jobs who were "trying to get back on their feet." These men and women were most likely recovering from drug and alcohol addiction or those who had seen the inside of a jail cell more times than they cared to remember.

On some occasions, my family would fear for my great-grandmother's safety because of her association with such people due to relapses, odd behaviors, and theft. Their protests were made apparent in their line of questioning, "Mama, why do you do it? Why do you want to be bothered with such people?" If you and I are honest, regarding those whose sins we can see with the naked eye, we often respond in this same judgmental manner, self-righteous even, with a "that's a not-of-God type of attitude." However, my great-grandmother would say in her southern accent, "Leave em' alone, they are just trying to make an honest living... someone has to help em' out."

When Mama went to be with the Lord, we recounted these stories and marveled at her love for the "least of these," the outcasts; those who people would not give a second glance, let alone allow them in their homes. I am encouraged by my great-grandmother's display of compassion and love, yet deeply challenged with the burning question: Am I willing to do the same?

I have often wondered why those who are ex-drug addicts, felons and other "bad sinners" (as if there is such a classification) are so graceful and seem to love God with a ferocious love. I sense a difference in their praise; it is almost palpable. It is love. It is their response to Love. The reason why some of us don't love others well is because we haven't fully grasped God's love. If I'll be honest, I tended to judge people harshly because that was how I judged myself and, furthermore, an extension of how I thought God responded to my sin and shame.

If you and I do not believe we have been granted full forgiveness—if we maintain this warped idea that we must work for it—we will not freely extend love and forgiveness to others. The mindset that "they don't deserve it" will become a stronghold in our hearts because deep down inside, we do not believe we deserve forgiveness any more than they do.

In this passage, we find a woman desperate to display her love for Jesus through pouring out a whole year's wages on His body. Unashamedly, she kisses Jesus' feet and washes it with her hair. Bear in mind, Jesus did not get his feet washed upon entering the home and sitting down for dinner (v 44). I will use my holy imagination and infer that our Savior's feet were dirty! Did that stop this woman? Nope, she understood the magnitude of the forgiveness that had been granted to her by Jesus. The men in the room were indignant because they had not yet grasped who they were sitting amongst and what Jesus could and would do for their souls.

I am reminded of the late Elisabeth Elliot's first husband's fateful death. While trying to witness to an indigenous community in Ecuador, he was murdered. With the strength of God, Elisabeth, a new mother, and widow forgave those people and continued the work her husband began. And do you know what happened?

Elisabeth's love in action coupled with the will to forgive what many of us would deem unacceptable and unforgivable, turned the hearts of many in that culture. They came to know Jesus because love begets love. Their hearts were so pricked because they understood those who are forgiven much, love much.

Prayer

Father God, I need You to help me grasp the great forgiveness I have been granted through the shed blood of Your Son Jesus on the cross at Calvary. I did not deserve Your forgiveness, yet in Your great love, You found a way for me to gain it through no effort of my own. For that, I will always be eternally grateful. Let those truths be a great reminder of how much I have been pardoned so that I can love all the more.

In Jesus name, Amen.

Today's Weapons

Luke 7:40-43

_____

_____

_____

_____

Exodus 34:6-7

_____

_____

_____

_____

Galatians 5:6

_____

_____

_____

_____

Your Turn

Sis, today is our last day together and in God's infinite wisdom and sense of humor, we find ourselves face to face with the foundation of our faith: forgiveness and love. It was the love of the Father that sent His only begotten Son to the cross that through His great sacrifice our sins would be forgiven. It amazes me how God works.

As I read over all the devos, I realize that a lot of the devos have been on love in some capacity or another and that is partly because I write from experience, but truth be told, I believe it is also because love is desperately lacking in the Christian community.

We are inundated with romantic fuzzy ideals of love but, in actuality, true love—Biblical love—looks and feels drastically different. True love is radical love!

To love like our Savior is risky; it is gritty, often painful, controversial even. It frequently requires forgiveness and acceptance of those who we deem unacceptable and the offense unforgivable.

On the last day, I simply ask that you reflect on two things:

Christ's love for you in that He would leave His heavenly dwelling, take on flesh, dwell amongst humans who would repeatedly sin against Him, and die so that you might be saved thousands of years later.

Your love for others.

How does one inform the other?

My Prayer For You

Father God,

You know my heart for your daughters. I want to see my sisters' whole, fully aware and assured of Your love for them and their ability to walk in their calling despite the distractions of the enemy.

I pray that their daily journey of Bible reading, and prayer does not end today. Ignite a fire within their bellies that leads them to seek You like never before. Embolden your daughters Lord. Hide Your Word in their hearts that they may not sin against You.

Lord remind them that Your divine power has already equipped them with everything they need to navigate life and maintain godliness. They have this privilege through the knowledge of You God, who called them by Your glory and goodness.

Protect my sisters O God. Meet them each at their point of need. For those reading this book and have never accepted Your Son Jesus as their personal Lord and Savior, speak to their hearts Lord. You love them and You have loved them since before the foundations of the Earth.

You sent Your only Son Jesus Christ to die for them while they were still sinners and could care less about Him. Help them believe that if they declare with their mouths that Jesus is Lord and believe that You raised Him from the dead, they will be saved. Resurrect dreams and restore lives God. Do what only You can do, and I will be so quick to give You all the glory You are due. Do it for Your Namesake.

In Jesus name, Amen.

Acknowledgements

Well, this was harder than I thought it would be. How does one acknowledge everyone without leaving anyone out? Simple, thank EVERYONE.

Thank you to everyone that had a part in the development of the woman that I am today. Thank you for your part in my story and subsequently these set of devos that originated from some of the toughest points of my life that yielded valuable lessons which molded my character.

A huge thank you to my editor, Noleen. You have been a Godsend every step of the way and in a whole other continent. I am so grateful for you.

Thank you, Mom and Dad, for the sacrifices you underwent as teenagers who found themselves in college and having a baby.

A big thank you to all my sibs, especially my only sissy, Alexus. I love each of you and I thank you for responding to my texts and voting on the intricate details of this book.

Thank you to my Yaya for recognizing the gift of writing within me when I couldn't see it for myself. Thank you for reminding me for the umpteenth time of the writing contest I won in grade school.

To my best friend, Alexis, thank you for making me feel like I can literally do anything God has called me to do. I love you!

Christina, thank you from the bottom of my heart for ALWAYS reading and proofreading my ideas. That English degree came in handy even if you are a nurse!

Mo, girl you read this manuscript when it was very much a work in progress, and for that I say thank you. I am grateful for your sisterhood, encouragement, and love.

To the most fashionable big cousin ever, Kelli, thank you for your input on each and every design option that I sent you. I am eternally grateful for your support.

To all my sisters in Christ, and you know who you are. I love you and I could not have done this without your prayers, kindness, words of encouragement, and truth.

Lastly, thank you God. The Only triune God who has never failed me. Thank you for infusing me with a great love of Your Word. You are so *so* good, and Your mercy endures forever.

About The Author

Adreeonah Mundy, a post-adoption specialist with an MA in Clinical Counseling Psychology, has spent the last 8 years on fire for God. She's made it her mission as a passionate Bible teacher, digital media specialist, mentor, and writer to teach biblical truths and strive to live them out in today's fast-paced society.

Her purpose is to teach and inspire God's children to live unashamedly for Christ so that He gets all the glory no matter the situation or circumstance. Adreeonah birthed the brand, "All Things Jesus." This YouTube and blog series was founded on the sheer desire to make Jesus famous and show fellow millennial women that you can, in fact, be fly and saved, culturally woke and yet not spiritually dead.

Love, fashion, job choices, relationships: Adreeonah has tackled it all and has created simple ways to not only keep the Word of God relevant but be a relatable and trusted ambassador of Jesus Christ while doing so.

Find out more *www.allthingsjesusmovement.com.*

Made in the USA
Monee, IL
29 January 2020

21013881R00105